Living as a Poor Person

The picture above has nothing to do with what I am about to share with you.

As a matter of fact, none of the pictures in this book relate to the content. The photos are included just to show off my photographs and as a distraction. When you get bored reading the contents, Just flip through the book and look at the pictures. Now you know.

Why would I do that? Because this little booklet is really about visualization; about imagination. We, people of modest means , are the way we are because we lack the funds to be rich. In short: we are poor because we have limited funds. Sometimes it is our fault but more than likely it is not. These are the facts of life.

So, even though this is all about living as a poor person as well as using our imagination, we have not lost sight of reality. We have to make do with our limited funds until we don't have to any more.

There. I said it.

I also want to alert you to the fact that this book is filled with grammatical errors and bad spelling. Have fun finding the errors and have fun with that.

A few days ago I went to Quickie-Mart and bought a loaf of Wheat Bread. I paid $2.99 for that bread. Later I went into a dollar store to buy cheap containers and saw wheat bread for $1. That's a big difference in price. The cashier told me that bread is delivered on Wednesdays. Now I know.

I share the above story because as a poor person you *MUST* always see everything in terms of value vs cost.

Let's assume that you are making $15 and hour. That is, you must spend 60 minutes of your limited and precious time to earn $15; time that you will never get back – It is that precious. That loaf of bread will either cost you 3 minutes of your time or 1 minute of your time. As a matter of fact, it is even more expensive than that after taxes. Think about that.

So, it is not stretch of the imagination to see that you must make your money stretch.

It is important, then, to see that money is life and when you cannot increase your income, you must increase its *value*.

Value. You must see everything having to do with money in terms of value. That is just the way it is.

I suggest strongly that in order to appreciate value in your life. You must see it for what it is.

The most valuable asset you have is you. YOU are the most important person in your life. Makes no difference if you are living in a tent or a mansion, you must see yourself as having value. That has a lot to do with self-respect. It has a lot to do with seeing yourself as being important. It has a lot to do with you taking time out each and every day to appreciate you as a person that is worth it.

First and foremost, you must erase a lifetime of mistaken beliefs. It is your beliefs that keep you from being successful. That's right; and I am not talking about having lots of money. I am talking about about being intelligent enough to use the funds you have to make the best of your life.

You must take very good look at what you believe to be true as opposed to what is nonsense and restrictive as afar as your growth is concerned.

Two of the most restrictive beliefs are the beliefs in ***Shame and Guilt.*** Get rid of them.

But, before you can do that, you must ***KNOW*** yourself. You are not what others say you are. You are you; that unique and special person. There must be that quest to know yourself.

Rule number one in life is to know yourself. That's it.

The quest to know yourself is the most important journey you will ever make in life. All the great Masters (sages) have one thing in common; From Buddha to Jesus, they all had to get away from the influence of the world and go on that quest for self-discovery. It may take you 40 hours, forty days, forty years or forty lifetimes but it is a quest you must make or chose to be a slave for the rest of your life. It is really that simple.

We are influenced my what we are told on a daily basis. We constantly bombarded with lies. Marketing appeals to our slave-mentality. We buy a pair of sneakers for 13 hours of our life when a pair of sneakers could have been obtain for just one hour of our life.

The quest for self-discovery is the most important quest you can ever make. Then and only then you can and will see life and living as it really is. No more false influences. No more beliefs in nonsense; no matter how appealing the worship of myths may seem. Once you know yourself then the second part comes into focus: To be TRUE to yourself. To be true to yourself.

Know yourself!
Be true to yourself!
It is very interesting that in the Bible, the first question God asked of mankind was , "Who told you..." Adam and Eve were naked in the Garden of Eden and they didn't realize that they were naked until they were told that they were naked. From then on they were influenced by others. Shame and guilt ruled their lives.
Shame and guilt.
Today, as I write this, the entire world will be celebrating Mothers Day. The world will be spending an extra $25Billion because we are told to celebrate Mothers' Day. Because I know who I am and because I am true to myself, it is my belief that everyday should be Mothers' Day. If you love your mother then you should not need to be told to celebrate the

love for your mother.

Yet, this holiday is popular because it imposes on guilt. Many people are a bit ashamed that they don't express their love more often.

I once witnessed my nephew buying his mother a BMW not because it was her birthday and not because it was Mothers' day but because he simply want to express his love and he could afford it. I was so impressed! Life is precious and your time is precious. Many people will be going deeper in debt because of marketing; and the exploitation of shame and guilt.

Of course, I could be wrong. What do you think?

I don't like Beets and I don't like Carrots. So, I don't buy them and I don't eat them. I do love mangoes! So, I buy and eat mangoes. That's me being true to myself.

Know yourself.

Be true to yourself.

By the way, When you know yourself and you then become a person who is true to yourself, you can expect to be ridiculed and shunned. You have now become that rare person that everyone wishes to be but is afraid to be.

There are a few reasons for that. The most important one is because of religion. (Which is NOT the same as believing in God). Chances are you were born into your religion; one of over 5000 different beliefs in a Gods created my mankind.

The plain truth is that religion is nonsense. But because we were born into our religion, we listen to others and continue to pretend that religion has value.

Who told you?

Every day on the news, you hear about the atrocities committed in the name of religion. Never fails. A place of worship is destroyed. Because of religion. Little children murdered because of religion. Wars and conflicts abound because of religion. People are starved because of religion. God demands human sacrifices because of religion. Groups of people are hated because of religion... Each religion justifying their acts of atrocities because of the scared book.

Once you know yourself and begin to be true for yourself, you then see the reality of things. You may even choose to adopt a belief in an Intelligent entity but that universal energy will be a one of your choice. T many people people it is called a spiritual awakening. Not a belief in a man-made "God" but an awareness that there is a universal and spiritual connection with all things and with all people... Or not. You choose what you believe or not believe in. Your belief, then, becomes, just as valid as anyone belief system.

Now what? Well, you have reached a stage in life when you are now thinking for yourself. The world is not very kind to free-thinkers. It is kind to the slave/master model and to those who cannot think for themselves.

OK. If you have read this far, it is now time to get real about personal blame. The truth is that many people are poor are will always be poor because they (as individuals) have created the conditions that invite poverty.

First their the big one: Cultivated attitude; meaning a bad attitude. Nobody wants to be around anyone with a bad attitude. It may look "macho" and it may be intended to intimidate, but the fact is that bad attitude repels employment. Come to an interview unprepared and with a bad attitude and you will almost always get the "Thank you for coming, but...". No good-paying job mean living in poverty. That's a fact.

The permanent frown and the look of the angry man or angry woman is a big no no. How many times have you gone into a grocery store and you greeted by the "angry look" of a cashier? That, too, is a projection of a seeming bad attitude. Without any extra effort on your part, go and look into a mirror. That face is what the entire world sees when they look at you. I made a video once where I emphasize that little thing called a smile. It was called "Smile first". Do yourself a favor and Google "Microdac Smile first video." The 2 minutes spent in watching that video is well worth it. I think so.

The old "Chip on the Shoulder" is another extremely bad way to present yourself to the world. That coupled with the "angry woman" or "angry man" attitude will not help in finding you the job you need to get out of poverty.

Unrelated, but I must ask. Do you like the above photo? I do. And here I want to mention something that may be keeping you in poverty: Your peers.

When I was a single man, a very wise woman once told me that for me the "right" woman, I had to be the "right" man. Those were some of the wisest words I have ever heard.

I worked at being the right man and I have been rewarded with the good fortune of being married to three of the most beautiful and kindest women in the world. Yes. I have been married and divorced three times; all to absolutely gorgeous women. [This little book is not about giving advice on marriage] By the way, if you really want to know why I have been married and divorced, just Google "microdac videos on marriage". But, that's another subject.

The point I wish to make here is this: Habit and your peers have a lot to do with you staying poor.

Consider for a moment that word "habit". Habit is what has caused you to be where you are in life. Habit. Habits are either good or bad. That's as simple as I can state that fact.

Cigarette smokers taught themselves to smoke, and then it became a habit. I smoked for 21 years. I did so because back in the 60's it was very cool to smoke cigarettes; everybody did it on TV and there was even the image of the Macho man who smoked. My first few cigarettes was agonizing – coughing and coughing – but I had to be cool. Being "cool" was a habit worth pursuing (or so I thought). Soon , in making myself smoke, it became a habit. I could only stop smoking by going through smoke cessation school. I had to learn to be a non-smoker. I had to develop new habits to take the place of the old. Get it. What habits are you still clinging to? What habits have you developed that are keeping you poor?   You taught yourself to drive a car, and now you can drive without even thinking about it. Driving is now a good habit. As I said, not all habits are bad habits. Let's face it, some habits are even very pleasant and have become extremely pleasurable.   Rich people who made it on their own, became rich because of habits they developed. Studying is a habit that pays big dissidents. Get it?

Before I get off the subject of habits, I would like to quote one the wisest author that I know of. Jesus, the son of Sirach (or maybe it was Solomon) on laziness.

Proverbs 13:4

"Lazy   people   want   much   but   get   little, but those who work hard will prosper."

So, what is one to do about replacing bad habits with habits that are good and pleasurable? There's but one answer and that is to simply do it.

Earlier, I made two points:

    (1) To Know yourself

    (2) To be true to yourself.

These two (of the 14 rules of Microdacism) are the most important two rules to live by. Microdacism? Yes. Google "Microdacism" to learn what I am talking about.

Mastering these two rules, through working hard at replacing bad habits, you then, in time become the human being that you were meant to me because now you can THINK FOR YOURSELF.

In thinking for yourself, you become very confident in your thoughts, visions and in your actions. You are no longer a slave to constant marketing techniques and shared nonsense.

In fact, when you think for yourself, you will see the flaws in many of my arguments and you will be confident in your own beliefs.

You will develop habits of reason and logic. You will no longer adopt the myths and stupidity that ordinary ignorant people find to be so comforting. You will know the truth in so many things and the truth will set you free.

In fact, and I am willing to make a small wager here, you will probably watch less TV and read a lot more. The daily propaganda will no longer have the effect on you that it once did. The nightly news with its subtle and constant suggestions of hate and fear will not longer have a hold on you.

In fact you will see no reason to hate the other guy because he is different, and you will read the so-called crime statistic and see that the occasional "bad salutation" is an abnormality and not the norm. You will soon come to realize that the "news" is so designed to frighten and to instill fear; tactics to sell products. But, that's another book.

The point is this: Maybe, when you think for yourself, being rich will take on a brand new meaning. Being rich may mean to have all your needs met as opposed to hoarding money. That's a revelation, isn't it? Thinking for yourself, then, brings you bliss and satisfaction.

Thinking for yourself becomes the ultimate habit!

It is my hope that by now you have come to realize that, for me, writing this book was share joy and was a fun project to showcase my photos.

This book is filled with errors and bad spelling. As a matter of fact, I expect that teachers everywhere will be encouraging their students to get this book and make the needed corrections as something fun to do.

I mean, why not have fun with this book?

So, who am I to have had the audacity to write a book? Just a guy who is loving life and being very grateful that I can do just that.

I say loving life because I am.

I get up every morning and thank that Universal Intelligence that created this amazing world of nature. I go for a walk as I mediate (which I do without having anything to do with religion). In meditating, I see myself as being Happy and contended and I am one with the world and with everyone.

I have no enemies.

I have sincere friend and relatives and I am mindful of being here and now. Life is simple for me. I have a bed to sleep in and it is comfortable. I have no need to have three or four beds. I have food to eat today and I have no need to have more food than I need. I have one bedroom and I have no need to have many bedrooms or a mansion.

I know the difference to have the use-of something and own something. So, I have no need to own anything or to impress anyone. I have more than adequate amount of food, clothing and shelter. I know the difference in "shopping"; the feeling of acquiring something and to "own" something. I then shop at thrift stores and get the thrill of shopping while living up to my mantra: Reuse, recycle, refurbish, regenerate, renew and make use of what is already here.

My lifestyle is definitely not for everyone. When you think for yourself, you develop your own lifestyle; one that suits you and nobody else.

It is not easy living a life that you have carved out of this world of constant bombardment.

You went through an education system that prepared you for employment and not necessarily for you to be a decent, ethical and good human being. Your educational system suggested strongly that there are Slaves and Masters. That there are workers and bosses. That there are servants and those to be served. Even your time is not your own. It is a 9 to 5 lifestyle and there's nothing you can do about it. In thinking for yourself you will develop a great sense of worth and self-respect. You will carve out a world to your liking and one that adheres to your ethics and principles. You may end up eating crackers instead of caviar, but the crackers are yours: paid for with funds within your means.

As you embrace your freedom to think for yourself, you might even be shunned by others. Your attitude of sharing and cooperating with others does not fit well in the mold of competing and being selfish.

Oh well. You may also take a track that is totally unique and different as you seek your own path.

So, you ask, what about these pictures?

Ok – so you didn't ask but I'll tell you just the same.

I take pictures and give them away free via my Facebook. Like my page. Facebook.com/microdac.

People use my pictures to make any picture project they wish and they then sell their projects for their organization, church or whatever... calenders, postcards, posters, etc. They go to my Facebook, then go to my photo album (there are over 600 pictures like these there) and they download whatever they wish. Why do I do that? Simple. Because I want to. I love sharing my work. All I ask is that the producer ask for my permission and that my pictures are not used to promote hate.

Yes. I do ask for donations because I I live on a fixed income. I use the funds to purchase cameras to take pictures and to make videos. You may enjoy and subscribe to my YouTube channel. Please do. YouTube.com/microdac.

My goal is to one day have channel where I can share Nature pictures and videos. I especially wish to share with those who are unable to go outdoors.

Google "Microdac Nature Channel" and do subscribe to my Private 4K nature channel.

It took me a while to reach this point in my life and I am happy.

Happy may be a very strong word, but, indeed, I am. I am at peace with myself and all my needs have been met.

But there's so much more to do!

I have been mentioning "Microdacism" and you may well be wondering what is it?

Microdacism is a set of 14 rules that I developed; rules to live by. It has since turned into a way of life. I hav already wrote about rule #1 and Rule #2. To know yourself and to be true to yourself.

Then there's rule #3:

"Develop friendships in a sincere and personal way, but, never forget that to others you are merely an asset or a liability. Beware of friendships that are based on the others' needs and not yours."

It may somewhat cynical but it is not. I am merely being practical. I'll share a little story to illustrate my point. I was invited to a party by a friend and my wife (at the time) asked out loud; who is being invited you, the person or the photographer? "Me, of course", I answered. My wife you is not only beautiful but wise beyond her years walked away with a smile. We got dressed and went to the party.

At the door I was greeted with the usual formalities and then the question:

"Did you bring your camera"?

Once you have taken the time to Know yourself and to be true to yourself, there are so many life changes that you will experience. You may even realize that many people are mere mimics and they go through life not having a clue as to who they. They are like characters on a stage. They are the stooges that they have been programmed to be and in their ignorance they have found their bliss.

Evaluating friends and friendships may become a challenge.

Identifying acquaintances may be a challenge.

Defining boundaries may become a challenge.

Truth and honesty may be challenging.

Sincerity and brutal honesty have become challenges.

You may spend time asking and defining what used to be acceptable in a lifestyle based on facades.

This is what I mean. Let's take relationships for example. We grew up in a world whereby on meeting someone we have to present ourselves with the "best foot forward". On going on a date, one is not allowed to be honest and to be one's SELF, but to be one's best. To go on a first date *"au natural"* guarantees a lack of success. So, that false first front becomes something to live up to in the relationship and the first signs of you being you is cause for disaster and a breakdown of the relationship. People in long-term realizations know that compromise is the key.

Then there's rule #4:

"Work to develop your intuitive and sensitive nature because those are the true engines of your creativity."

Two stories:

I once played golf with a Medical Doctor (Retired) that is regret in life is that he didn't pursue his first love: Working with wood. What? He said that after many failed marriages and lots of money in alimony payment to his ex wives, he thinks that had he become a wood-worker he would have been happier about life and living.

He regretted not going after his creative pursuits.

But, he said, his parents wanted him to be a doctor. It was their dream that he became a doctor. Their joy was in their frequent chats about their son"the doctor". Do you know anyone like that?

The other story is in knowing creative people. The ones who, at an early age, knew what they wanted to do with their lives. To teach, to act, to dance, to paint, to make wooden things, to build houses, to be gardeners, to work in food banks... to make a difference in this world. They all, collectively, were the happiest people; not rich but they were people who were fulfilled and happy with their choices. They followed their intuitive and sensitive nature. Money is not everything. Money is what we use to acquire what we need. That's it and should be a goal.

As for rule #5 (and I won't go through all the so-called rules). It states simply:

"In your personal life, do what you do for self satisfaction and never for approval, which is a poor slave master. Applause and approval from others can be insincere. You doing your best at whatever who choose is always the ultimate goal."

I once met a woman who was very angry and bitter about life in general and about her life in particular. She had spent all of her adult life taking care of her mother who, in turn, pursued religious studies. No boyfriends, no meaningful relationships.

Another woman I know of died in her 60's as a well educated woman who died alone and as a virgin; not because she wanted to remain a virgin, but because no man was good enough for her. She was so judgmental that no one from her family (much less friends) came to he funeral.

Another woman I know is very bitter about who she was treated by her mother. All her life she felt unloved. Her Mother, in the mean time, in her late eighties, is a millionaire and is till uncaring to her daughter. Her mom's ego continues to be a major part of her life and she will leave her fortune to a foundation that will bear her name (and not to her daughter). How sad. There are many stories like these.

One must live one's own life for one's own happiness.

I always feel a little sad when I hear from people who sacrificed their happiness for someone else. On the surface it appears to be so noble, but, why is one life more important than another?

To me, self-satisfaction in every form is the way to go. How can one person say that love another if they don't love themselves first and foremost? On what do they base their love? Can one be sensual and sharing with another without knowing what it means personally?

Self-satisfaction, to me, is one of the greatest joys of life.

These pictures that I share, I do so willingly because I find great satisfaction in sharing with others... in every way.

A woman I know was giving a beautiful silk spread that was made in old China. She took great pride in owning such a treasure that she locked it away for years. Then one day, the woman who had given the spread wanted to know why was it not on her bed. It wasn't on her bed, she said, because she had locked it away to keep it safe.

When the woman opened the box where the spread was kept, all she found was dust and the many moths that flew out of the box. Had she used the spread she would have had some satisfaction.

I share my pictures because it gives me great satisfaction in sharing what I have. I am happy to say that sharing has become a part of what makes me very happy.

The 6th rule in Microdacism is one that I site quite often:
"Create something each and every day."

I do my best to live up to this rule (As my Facebook friends will attest). I am very old now. Lots of memories and unable to do what I used to be able to do.

Exercise wise, I try to walk each and every day, but, if truth be told, I not always able to do so. Today, I did walk over two miles as I took pictures (some of which I am sharing here). I also try my best to play at least nine holes of golf – walking as I carry my bag.

But, when it comes to photography, I try not to miss taking pictures each and every day. That, to m, is fulfilling my self-imposed obligation of creating something each and every day.

The pictures you have been seeing were shots with one of three cameras. A Canon T3i (or T4i), A Panasonic FZ1000 and/or a Panasonic ZS70. I shoot mostly in 4K because I want my pictures to be enjoyed for a long time. My 4K Nature videos are being enjoyed in some 200 countries. I like that.

And, yes, I keep buying lotto tickets (maybe once a month) because I want a 4.6K video camera. It is very expensive. I keep thinking that one of these days a rich person will enjoy sharing their wealth...

The 7th rule was inspired by the 2nd rule:

"Be Yourself always. Others will either like you or not like you based on their need for having you in their life."

My nieces and nephews call me "UD"; short for Uncle Dave. I cannot begin to tell you the pride and joy I feel being around them all. I know what I feel having them in my life. I consider myself to be blessed beyond words to be in their lives.

My own children are amazing also, and I truly blessed to have had the great honor to be their father.

When I am around my relatives and friends, I give the courtesy of being myself in their company. Being me they then can see and appreciate who and what I am. I have no need for a charade.

And, here's the thing that is important. I love them all not because of how they feel about me me, but, because of how how I feel about them. Nobody can know the mind of another, but I can relate to you how I feel.

To repeat: In being myself around others I am respecting them as fellow human beings worthy of my honesty in being.

I am.

What you see is who and what I am.

If you have read this far, what must be painfully obvious to you is that I am not a writer. I have no education in being a writer. But, I do write. I have fun doing this.

I very thoughtful reader of one of my $1 ebooks wrote me a very long email being very critical of my work. He was sincere and I appreciate the fact that he had invested $1 to read what I wrote. [As a matter of fact – I make $0.38 for every $1 you spend in purchasing my books]. This book, as you can see is more than $1.00.

Anyway, I answered te thoughtful reader and thanked him for his time to read my book and I was very sincere in stating that his kindness in educating me was not lost on me.

Look, I believe that many people remain poor in cash, in spirit and in heart because of FEAR. Fear is very crippling. Fear is what makes people cling to beliefs that they know are wrong.

Fear of success. Fear of failure. Fear of being criticized. Fear of not being liked. Fear of not having enough when one is surrounded by plenty.

Fear of being poor when you have access to so much!

Fear, I think, is what keep many clinging to the illusion of poverty. Being so-called poor is not always a fact but an illusion.

I have a question:

How much respect do you have for a man or a woman who has billions of dollars and do nothing with their money to eliminate starvation?

Only you can answer that question.

As for me. I have more respect for the man at McDonalds who took his last $10.00 and helped to buy food for the lady with the three kids. He bought two items from the dollar menu and told the cashier to buy some food for the kids that he didn't know.

Perhaps my question was not a fair question because, in truth, I don't envy people with lots of money. In fairness, I do read that many super-rich spend their money on projects that only the super rich can do; such as eliminating malaria in Africa.

I am just grateful that I am in a position to have my needs met without compromising my visions. My visions include having better cameras. Who knows, maybe you, the reader will get me that 4.6K camera and complete kit.

But, about being poor. Maybe the answers is within you. That is, improve what you control: Your education, attitude and your personality,. Be prepared. Luck, you see, is being prepared for opportunity when it comes knocking.

MICRODACISM

1. The quest for *self discovery* is the **_MOST_** important quest in life.

2. **_KNOWING yourself_** and being ***true to yourself*** is the most important way to live.

3. Develop friendships in a sincere and personal way, but, never forget that to others you are merely an asset or a liability. The friendship could well be based on their needs and not yours.

4. Work to develop your intuitive and sensitive nature because those are the true engines of your creativity.

5. In your personal life, do what you do for self satisfaction and never for approval which is a poor slave master. Applause and criticism are insincere at best.

6. Create something each and every day!

7. Be yourself always. Others will either like you or not based on their need for having you in their life. Lower your expectation of others and you wont be disappointed.

8. Generosity and sharing are not what you do for others. It is what you do for yourself. It is one of the most important of all the spiritual laws. When you give or share, do so without strings attached.

9. Happiness is directly related to one's dependence on others (or things). The less dependent you are of others, the happier you are.

10. Your belief in God is a personal matter. Keep it to yourself. Finding and recognizing God is a personal quest and to each it is different.

11. Your discovery of spiritual laws is your discovery. Extend the courtesy of allowing others to make their own discovery. Note: These laws are not in books; holy or otherwise.

12. Hurt no one in any way, but always be aware that is not the way of all people, so, always have a plan "B".

13. Learn to accept from others. They give for THEIR own reasons (Not yours). The Master pays. The servant is the one who receives. Know your place in the lives of others.

14. In your professional life, do what you do because you want to to do what you do and not for thank-you or for applause. The Master pays and the servant accepts payment. Whether you do with a good attitude or a bad attitude, you have spent time that can never be replaced.

Think for yourself.

Microdac Videos
microdac@msn.com

www.microdac.com
www.facebook.com/microdac
www.youtube.com/microdac.com

Stay Focused

THINK
For
YOURSELF

Do it anyway In spite of your Fear

www.ingramcontent.com/pod-product-compliance
Lightning Source LLC
Chambersburg PA
CBHW041211180526
45172CB00006B/1238